Melting, Freezing, and Boiling Science Projects with Matter

Robert Gardner

Enslow Elementary

an imprint of

 Enslow Publishers, Inc.

40 Industrial Road
Box 398
Berkeley Heights, NJ 07922
USA

http://www.enslow.com

J
507.8
Bar

Enslow Elementary, an imprint of Enslow Publishers, Inc.

Enslow Elementary® is a registered trademark of Enslow Publishers, Inc.

Library of Congress Cataloging-in-Publication Data

Gardner, Robert, 1929–
Melting, freezing, and boiling science projects with matter / Robert Gardner.
    p. cm. — (Fantastic physical science experiments)
Includes bibliographical references and index.
ISBN-10: 0-7660-2589-6
    1. Matter—Properties—Experiments—Juvenile literature.
2. Temperature—Experiments—Juvenile literature. I. Title.
    QC173.36.G368 2006
    507'.8—dc22   2005033753

ISBN-13: 978-0-7660-2589-9

Printed in the United States of America

10 9 8 7 6 5 4 3 2

To Our Readers: We have done our best to make sure all Internet Addresses in this book were active and appropriate when we went to press. However, the author and the publisher have no control over and assume no liability for the material available on those Internet sites or on other Web sites they may link to. Any comments or suggestions can be sent by e-mail to comments@enslow.com or to the address on the back cover.

Illustration credits: Tom LaBaff

Cover illustration: Tom LaBaff

Contents

(Experiments with a 🎗 symbol feature **Ideas for Your Science Fair**.)

Introduction

You, the world, and everything in the entire universe are made of matter. The tiniest bits of matter are atoms and molecules. They are much too small to be seen. A billion trillion of them together make up a tiny bit of a solid or liquid that we can hardly see. Most gases are colorless. We can't see them because their molecules are very far apart. But we can feel one gas—air. It pushes against us when it is windy. And we feel it when we run or ride a bicycle.

Doing the experiments in this book will help you unlock some of the secrets of matter. You will understand why solids sometimes disappear, why there are gaps in railroad tracks, how thermometers work, and much, much more.

Entering a Science Fair

All of the experiments in this book are followed by ideas for science fair projects. However, judges at science fairs like experiments that are creative. So do not simply copy an experiment from this book. Expand on one of the ideas suggested, or think of a project of your own. Choose a topic you really like and want to know more about. Then your project will be more interesting to you. Your curiosity can lead to a creative experiment that you plan and carry out.

Before entering a science fair, read one or more of the books listed under Further Reading. They will give you helpful hints and lots of useful information about science fairs.

Safety First

To do experiments safely, always follow these rules:

1. Do all experiments under adult supervision.

2. Read all instructions carefully. If you have questions, check with the adult.

3. Be serious when experimenting. Fooling around can be dangerous to you and to others.

4. Keep the area where you work clean and organized. When you have finished, clean up and put materials away.

5. Never experiment with electric wall outlets.

6. When doing these experiments, use only non-mercury thermometers, such as those filled with alcohol. The liquid in some thermometers is mercury. It is dangerous to breathe mercury vapor. If you have mercury thermometers, **ask an adult** to take them to a local mercury thermometer exchange location.

1. From Solid to Liquid to

Matter is anything that has weight. Matter can be a solid, a liquid, or a gas. Ice cubes are solids. Like all solids, ice cubes have a certain size and shape.

Let's Begin!

Things you will need:
- ✔ an adult
- ✔ safety glasses
- ✔ ice cubes
- ✔ small cooking pan
- ✔ stove
- ✔ cold water
- ✔ glass vessel such as Pyrex glass coffee pot
- ✔ oven mitts
- ✔ 1-gallon, clear plastic bag that can be sealed (Those with a one-zip slider work well.)
- ✔ microwave oven with window
- ✔ large syringe without a needle
- ✔ a solid, such as a wooden block

Put on safety glasses. You will be near heated substances that might spatter.

1. Put four ice cubes into a small pan. **Ask an adult** to *gently* heat the pan on a stove. What happens to the ice?

   Does liquid water have a certain shape?

2. Have the **adult** continue heating the pan. After a while, do bubbles of gas begin rising in the liquid? What happens when they

Gas and Back

reach the surface? The liquid is boiling. It is changing to an invisible gas (steam).

❸ Pour a cup of cold water into a glass container. **Ask the adult**, wearing oven mitts, to hold the container above the boiling water. What collects on the bottom of the glass? What do you think is happening?

❹ **Have the adult** continue heating the pan for a while. As you can see, it would take a long time to change all the liquid to a gas. What does this tell you? Is a lot of heat needed to change liquid water to a gas?

How could you change liquid water into a solid?

cold water

boiling water

You can show that boiling water really changes into a gas.

⑤ Find a one-gallon, clear plastic bag that can be sealed. Put an ice cube in the bag. To get all the air out of the bag, flatten and roll it. Then seal the bag so that nothing can get in or out.

⑥ Place the bag in a microwave oven. **Have an adult** turn on the oven for 20-second intervals. Watch what happens through the window. How much time is needed to melt the ice? How much time passes before the water begins to boil? What happens to the volume as the water boils? How can you tell? **Do not touch the bag; let it cool.**

⑦ Stop heating when the bag is full. Keep the oven closed for several minutes. What happens as the gas cools?

⑧ Pull the piston of a large syringe (without a needle) partway out. This will draw air into the cylinder. Put your finger firmly over the open end of the syringe. Push the piston inward. Can you squeeze (compress)

the gas into a smaller space? Can you make the volume bigger by pulling the piston outward?

9 Can you compress a liquid into a smaller volume? Use your syringe to find out.

Can you compress a solid, such as a wooden block?

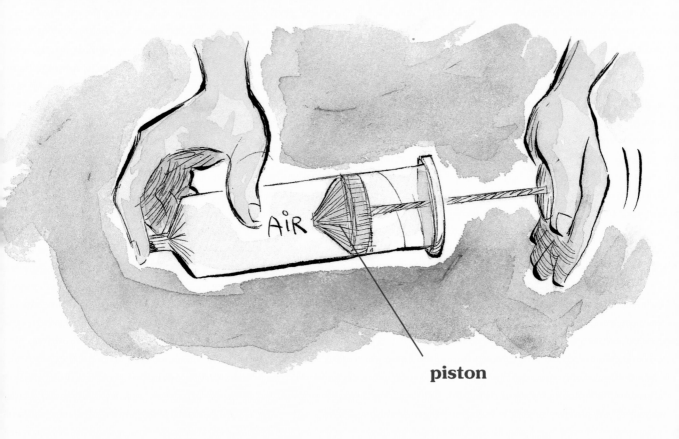

piston

From Solid to Liquid to Gas

Ice is solid water. Heat flowed from the stove to the pan and then to the ice. The heat melted the ice. (The ice changed from a solid to a liquid.)

Ice melts slowly. It takes some heat to raise the temperature of some water one degree Celsius (1.8 degrees Fahrenheit). It takes 80 times as much heat to melt the same amount of ice.

After melting, the ice is a liquid. Its shape can change. It takes the shape of the container it is in.

The water in the pot boiled. It was changing from a liquid to a gas. The bursting bubbles you saw were gas bubbles (steam). Steam is water that has become

and Back: An Explanation

a gas. The hot gas (steam) bumped into a cold surface (the glass container with cold water). The gas lost heat. It changed back to a liquid. We say the gas *condensed*.

It takes a long time to change liquid water to a gas (steam). Why? Because lots of heat is needed to change liquid water to steam. It takes some heat to warm melted ice to the temperature at which the water boils. It takes about 5 ½ times as much heat to change the boiling water to steam.

Changing liquid water to a solid (ice) is easy. Put a container of water in a freezer. Leave it for several hours. You will see that the liquid becomes a solid.

You heated the ice in a sealed bag. A gas formed in the bag when the water boiled. The bag filled up with gas (steam). When it cooled, the gas condensed. Its volume decreased. The bag shrank.

You easily squeezed (compressed) the gas (air) in the syringe into a smaller volume. And you could make its volume bigger by pulling the piston outward.

You could pull water into the syringe. You tried to squeeze the water into a smaller space. But you found the liquid could not be compressed. And, no matter how hard you push on most solids, they will not shrink.

Ideas for Your Science Fair

★ Do an experiment to find out at what temperature water changes to a solid (ice).
★ **Under adult supervision,** do an experiment to find out at what temperature water changes to a gas (steam).

2. Water Holds Together

Liquid water has interesting properties. One such property is the way it holds together.

Let's Begin!

① Find three clean medicine cups (or pill vials). Do the cups need to be washed? If they do, rinse them thoroughly with running water.

② Fill one cup to the very top with water. Using an eyedropper, continue to add water drop by drop. Can you heap water above the top of the cup? How many drops can you add before water runs over the edge?

③ Place a second, identical cup beside the one with water. Repeat the experiment, but use rubbing alcohol instead of water. Can you heap alcohol as high as water?

④ Stir several drops of liquid soap into a glass of water. Repeat the experiment by adding soapy water to a third identical cup. Can you heap soapy water as high as water? As high as alcohol?

Water holds together so well that it seems to have a skin.

⑤ Nearly fill a clean, wide, well-rinsed plastic container with water. Using a dinner fork, gently lay a paper clip on the water. Can you see the dimples in the water's "skin"?

⑥ Predict what will happen if you add a drop of soap to the water. Try it! Were you right?

water

Water Holds Together:

Water holds together very well. Why? Because water molecules have a strong pull toward each other. They pull together so well that water can go against gravity. It can heap up well above the lip of a cup and not fall out. Water molecules pull together so strongly they create a skinlike surface. This "skin" can stop paper clips and needles, placed flat, from sinking through the water's surface.

Alcohol and soapy water do not hold together as well as water. Adding even a drop of soap breaks the water's skin. The soap molecules get between the water molecules. This reduces the strong pull between each of the water molecules. The soapy water will not hold up the paper clip.

As you found in Experiment 1, it takes lots of heat to separate water molecules. That is because the molecules hold together so strongly. Gas molecules are far apart; liquid molecules are very close together. When a liquid changes to a gas, the molecules move apart. The space the gas molecules take up increases about a thousand times. Separating molecules is like lifting weights against gravity. It takes a lot of energy.

An Explanation

It takes a lot of heat energy to separate molecules of water to form a gas (steam).

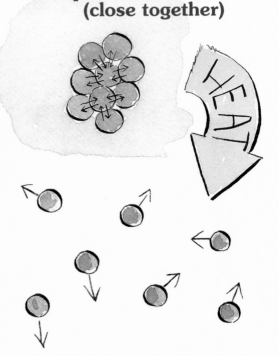

**liquid water molecule
(close together)**

**gaseous water molecule
(far apart)**

Idea for Your Science Fair

★ Do an experiment to show that a force is needed to separate water.

3. Disappearing

Can liquids disappear without boiling? You can do an experiment to find out.

Let's Begin!

Things you will need:
- ✔ 2 saucers
- ✔ water (hot and cold)
- ✔ rubbing alcohol
- ✔ paper towels
- ✔ clothespins
- ✔ clothesline
- ✔ electric fan
- ✔ 2 open cardboard boxes

1 Cover the bottom of a saucer with water. Cover the bottom of a second saucer with rubbing alcohol. Leave the saucers in a warm (not hot) place for several days. Do the liquids slowly disappear? If so, we say the liquids evaporate. Which liquid evaporated first?

2 Soak a paper towel in hot tap water. Soak an identical towel in cold water. Use clothespins to hang both towels on the same clothesline. Which towel dries faster? How does temperature affect evaporation?

3 Soak two identical paper towels in cold water. Fold one towel again and again until it is a small rectangle. Leave the second towel unfolded. Hang both towels

on the same clothesline. Which towel dries faster? How does the amount of surface touching the air affect evaporation?

④ Soak two identical paper towels in the same water. Hang each towel from separate open cardboard boxes. Use a fan to blow air across one towel but not the other. Which towel dries first? How does wind affect evaporation?

Explain why you think each of the things you tested—temperature, amount of surface, and wind—affects how fast water evaporates.

clothespin

cardboard boxes
open at both ends

water

alcohol

Disappearing Liquids:

Molecules are always moving. Some move faster than others. Temperature measures the average speed of the molecules. The hotter a substance, the faster its molecules move. Some fast-moving liquid molecules can overcome the forces that hold them together. These faster molecules escape. They become a gas and mix with molecules of air. Alcohol evaporates faster than water. The forces holding alcohol together are not as strong as those holding water together.

Water in the hot towel evaporated faster than water in the cold towel. Hot water evaporates faster than cold water. The average hot-water molecule moves faster than the average cold-water molecule. More hot-water (faster) molecules break apart and become a gas.

The spread-out towel dried faster than the folded one. Fast-moving molecules exposed to air can escape from the liquid (evaporate). Molecules that are not exposed bump into other water molecules. They remain a liquid. The more wet towel that is exposed to air, the faster the evaporation.

An Explanation

The towel in the wind dried faster than the towel in still air. Wind carries away water molecules that have become a gas. Without wind, some of the escaping molecules get bumped back into the towel. They become liquid again.

Fast-moving molecules may become a gas. Slower molecules are left in the liquid.

Hot Wet Towel

Ideas for Your Science Fair

- ★ Do an experiment to show that evaporation causes a liquid to cool.
- ★ Do an experiment to show what happens when salt water evaporates. Try to explain what you observe.

4. Making Solids

As you have seen, liquids may disappear. They boil or evaporate and become a gas. Can you make a solid disappear?

Let's Find Out!

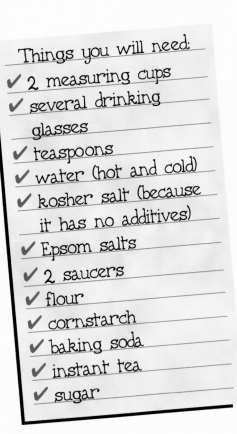

Things you will need:
- ✔ 2 measuring cups
- ✔ several drinking glasses
- ✔ teaspoons
- ✔ water (hot and cold)
- ✔ kosher salt (because it has no additives)
- ✔ Epsom salts
- ✔ 2 saucers
- ✔ flour
- ✔ cornstarch
- ✔ baking soda
- ✔ instant tea
- ✔ sugar

❶ Find a measuring cup. Then pour 60 mL (2 ounces) of water into each of 2 glasses.

❷ Add a level teaspoon of kosher salt to the water in one glass. Add a level teaspoon of Epsom salts to the water in the other glass. Stir the two solid-liquid mixtures. Do the solids disappear? If the solids disappear, we say they have *dissolved* in the water. The dissolved solid in the liquid is a *solution*.

❸ Can you make the solids reappear? Pour a little of

Disappear

each solution into separate saucers. Leave the saucers in a warm (not hot) place for several days. Do you think the solids will reappear?

④ Try dissolving flour, cornstarch, baking soda, and instant tea in separate glasses of water. Do all these solids disappear?

⑤ Add $\frac{1}{2}$ cup of warm water to a measuring cup. Pour $\frac{1}{4}$ cup of sugar into the water in the measuring cup. Stir to make the sugar disappear. Do you have $\frac{3}{4}$ cup of sugar solution? Why or why not?

kosher
salt

Epsom
salts

Making Solids Disappear:

Epsom salt, kosher salt, and sugar disappear when mixed with water. The solids *dissolve* in the liquid to make *solutions*.

When a solution forms, molecules of solid fit between molecules of liquid. Together they form a transparent liquid—the solution. Molecules are too small to be seen. Therefore, the solid disappears when its molecules separate in the liquid. At room temperature, about 20 grams ($7/10$ ounce) of both Epsom and kosher salt will dissolve in 2 ounces of water. Nearly four times as much sugar will dissolve in that much water.

The $1/2$ cup of water and $1/4$ cup of sugar do not form $3/4$ cup of solution! The sugar molecules fit into spaces between the water molecules. The volume of the solution is just a little more than the volume of the water. If the water evaporates, the solid will be left.

Not all solids dissolve in water. Flour and cornstarch do not disappear when mixed with water. These two solids, and many others, do not dissolve in water. We say they are insoluble in water.

An Explanation

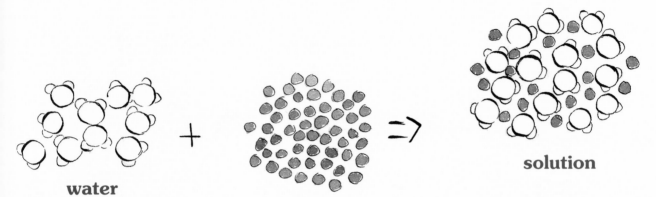

water + sugar => solution

Ideas for Your Science Fair

★ How does the temperature of the water affect the solubility of Epsom salts? Of kosher salt? Of sugar? Do experiments to find out.

★ Will Epsom salts, kosher salt, and sugar dissolve in alcohol? In vinegar?

5. Making a Gas

Gases can be made by heating liquids until they boil. But gases can also be made by mixing certain chemicals.

Let's Begin!

Things you will need:
- ✔ an adult
- ✔ water
- ✔ measuring cup
- ✔ 8-oz plastic or glass bottle with a mouth about 1 in. wide
- ✔ 4 seltzer tablets
- ✔ round balloon about 4 in. long and 2 in. wide when deflated
- ✔ clay
- ✔ birthday candle
- ✔ short drinking glass about 3-4 in. tall
- ✔ matches

❶ Add 2 ounces of water to a measuring cup. Pour the water into an 8-ounce plastic or glass bottle.

❷ Break two seltzer tablets. Quickly drop them into the bottle. **Have an adult** quickly pull the mouth of a balloon over the top of the bottle. What is happening in the bottle? What is happening to the balloon?

❸ Find a short drinking glass. Use clay to support a birthday candle on the bottom of the glass. **Ask an adult** to light the candle. Pour 2 ounces of water into the glass. Be careful! Don't put out the candle.

4 Add two broken seltzer tablets to the glass. What happens to the candle as the gas collects in the glass?

The gas you made is found in many fire extinguishers. What gas do you think it is?

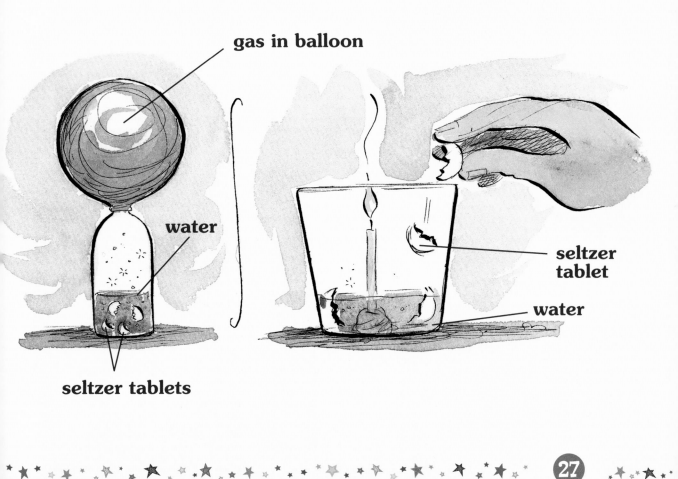

gas in balloon

water

seltzer tablets

seltzer tablet

water

Making a Gas:

Seltzer tablets contain citric acid and baking soda. When they are put in water, the acid and baking soda combine to make a gas. The fizzing you saw was many bubbles of carbon dioxide gas. The carbon dioxide pushed the air out of the bottle. It then filled the bottle and the attached balloon.

Many fire extinguishers contain carbon dioxide because things cannot burn in the gas. Some fire extinguishers produce the gas chemically as you did.

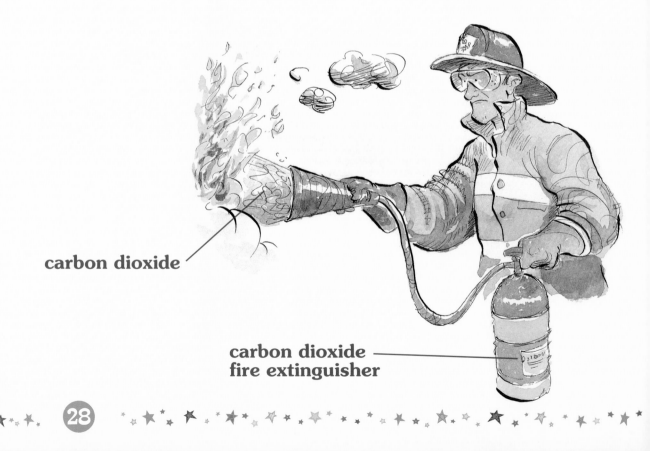

carbon dioxide

carbon dioxide
fire extinguisher

An Explanation

A liter of carbon dioxide is heavier than a liter of air. You made the gas by adding seltzer to water in an open glass. The carbon dioxide stayed in the glass. You know that metal coins sink in water. In the same way, carbon dioxide sinks in air. The heavy gas gradually filled the space around the burning candle. It pushed the air up and out of the glass. Because things cannot burn in carbon dioxide, the flame went out.

Ideas for Your Science Fair

★ Can you find a way to make soap bubbles float on carbon dioxide?

★ Adding carbon dioxide to limewater makes the limewater turn milky. (You may be able to borrow some limewater from your school's science teacher.) Use this fact to test whether the gas you exhale contains carbon dioxide.

6. Expansion and

What happens to a gas when it is heated or cooled?

Let's Find Out!

1. In a sink, nearly fill a dishpan with cold water. Put the open mouth of an empty 2-L plastic soda bottle under the water. Hold the bottle in your warm hands. Be careful not to squeeze the bottle. Why do you think bubbles of gas (air) come out of the bottle?

2. Let a stream of cold water flow over its outside surface. This will cool the bottle. Then ask **an adult** to slip the mouth of a balloon over the open end of the empty bottle.

3. Warm the gas in the bottle. Hold the bottle under a stream of hot water. Be careful not to squeeze the bottle. What happens to the balloon? What does this tell you?

4. Put the bottle and attached balloon in a refrigerator. After 20 minutes, look at the bottle. What has happened? What does this tell you?

Contraction of Gases

⑤ Next, put the bottle in a freezer. Wait 20 minutes. Then look at the bottle and attached balloon again. Can you explain what has happened?

⑥ Remove the bottle and attached balloon from the freezer. Leave them in a warm room. Predict what will happen. Were you right?

Things you will need:
- ✓ an adult
- ✓ an empty 2-L plastic soda bottle
- ✓ sink with cold and hot water faucets
- ✓ dishpan
- ✓ balloon
- ✓ refrigerator
- ✓ clock or watch
- ✓ freezer

hot water

soda bottle

balloon

Expansion and Contraction

All gases expand (spread out) when heated. That is why bubbles of air came out of the bottle. Your warm hands heated the air in the bottle. This made the air expand. The expanding air came out of the bottle. It had nowhere else to go. Running hot water over the bottle added more heat to the air inside. The warm air expanded into the balloon. It filled the balloon with air.

All gases contract (get smaller) when cooled. When you put the bottle in the refrigerator, the gas contracted. The balloon shrank. Putting the bottle in a freezer made the gas contract even more. It may have caused the sides of the bottle to cave in. The balloon was empty, so it may even have pulled the balloon into the bottle.

Putting the bottle back into a warm room made the gas expand again. The bottle and balloon returned to their original size. You may have predicted that this would happen.

Warm gas molecules move faster than cooler molecules. Because they move faster, they take up more room. Removing heat makes gas molecules slow down. Slower molecules take up less space.

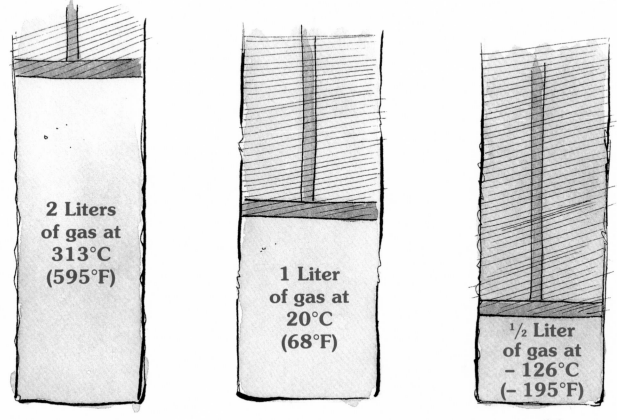

2 Liters of gas at 313°C (595°F)

hot

1 Liter of gas at 20°C (68°F)

warm

½ Liter of gas at −126°C (−195°F)

cold

Ideas for Your Science Fair

★ Do an experiment to show that carbon dioxide expands and contracts in the same way as air.

★ Show that other gases such as oxygen, nitrogen, and helium expand and contract in the same way as air.

7. Expansion and

Do liquids expand and contract? You can do an experiment to find out.

Let's Find Out!

Things you will need:
- ✔ an adult
- ✔ small alcohol thermometer with a range of about -10 to 50°C (10 to 120°F)
- ✔ ice cube
- ✔ narrow glass tube
- ✔ one-hole cork or rubber stopper
- ✔ soap
- ✔ test tube
- ✔ food coloring
- ✔ water
- ✔ felt-tip pen
- ✔ cooking pan
- ✔ hot water
- ✔ glass of ice water (You may be able to borrow some of these things from your science teacher)

❶ Put your thumb on the bulb (bottom) of an alcohol thermometer. What happens to the liquid in the bulb?

❷ Put an ice cube on the bulb. What happens?

❸ **Ask an adult** to put one end of a narrow glass tube into a one-hole cork or rubber stopper. (A little soap on the glass will help it slide into the cork or stopper.)

❹ Fill a test tube brim-full of colored water. Push the cork or rubber stopper into the tube. The colored water should rise partway up the glass tube and stay there.

Contraction of a Liquid

⑤ Mark the water level in the glass tube with a felt-tip pen.

⑥ **Have an adult** hold the test tube in a pan of hot water. What happens to the water level in the narrow tube as the water in the test tube warms? What does this tell you?

⑦ **Have the adult** remove the test tube from the pan. Let the water level return to the mark you made. Then put the test tube in a glass of ice water. What happens to the water level in the glass tube? Why do you think this happened?

mark on glass

cork or rubber stopper

colored water

hot water

Expansion and Contraction

Heating a liquid makes the molecules move faster. But liquid molecules, unlike gas molecules, are close together. Think of them as dancers filling a crowded dance floor. As long as the music is slow, the dancers have room. But suppose the music speeds up. Then some of the fast-moving dancers will be bumped off the floor. They use more space as they dance around. In the same way, a liquid expands when heated. However, liquids expand much less than gases for the same rise in temperature.

The alcohol (a liquid) in the thermometer expanded when heated by your thumb. It looked like it expanded a lot because it was going up a very narrow tube. The liquid contracted when you cooled it with ice.

Water also expands when heated. It contracts when cooled. You saw that this was true with the water thermometer you made. When the water was heated, it rose up the tube. When the water cooled, the water level dropped. The liquid contracted.

# of a Liquid: An Explanation

Colder, slower molecules take up less space.

Warmer, faster molecules take up more space.

Idea for Your Science Fair

★ Water, unlike most liquids, expands when it freezes. Do an experiment to show that water expands when it changes to a solid (ice). How does this explain why it floats in water?

8. Expansion and

Engineers leave small spaces between lengths of railroad tracks. They do the same for sections of steel bridges. This is a hint that solids also expand and contract. Do they?

Let's Find Out!

Things you will need:
- ✔ an adult
- ✔ bare 20-24 gauge copper or aluminum wire at least 2 meters (6½ feet) long (available at a hardware store)
- ✔ hook in ceiling of basement or garage
- ✔ weight
- ✔ pointer made from lightweight cardboard
- ✔ scissors
- ✔ tape
- ✔ heavier cardboard
- ✔ marking pen
- ✔ multipurpose butane lighter

1. Obtain a piece of copper or aluminum wire at least 2 meters (6½ feet) long. Attach one end of the wire to a high hook in the ceiling of a basement or garage. Attach the lower end to a weight. This will straighten the wire. Leave a small distance between the floor and the bottom of the weight.

2. Make a pointer from a small piece of lightweight cardboard. Tape it to the bottom of the wire as shown.

Contraction of a Solid

③ Stand a folded piece of heavier cardboard next to the pointer. With a marking pen, draw a line on the heavy cardboard at the end of the pointer.

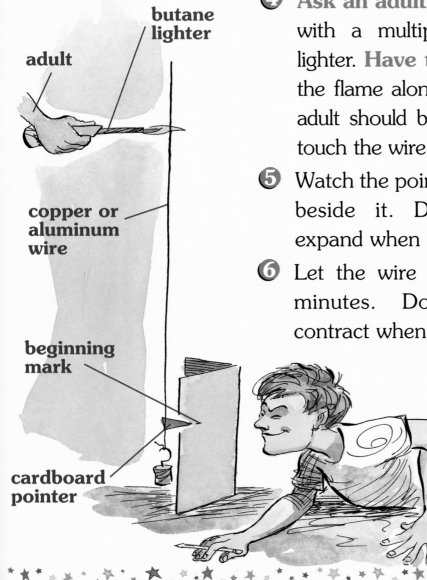

butane lighter

adult

copper or aluminum wire

beginning mark

cardboard pointer

④ **Ask an adult** to heat the wire with a multipurpose butane lighter. **Have the adult** move the flame along the wire. The adult should be careful not to touch the wire with the lighter.

⑤ Watch the pointer and the line beside it. Does the wire expand when heated?

⑥ Let the wire cool for a few minutes. Does the wire contract when it cools?

Expansion and Contraction

As you saw, a solid metal wire expands very little when heated. A hot flame was needed to see any expansion at all. Suppose you have a copper wire 10 meters (33 feet) long. It will expand only 1.7 centimeters when its temperature rises 100 degrees Celsius (180 degrees Fahrenheit).

The wire contracted to its original length when it cooled. You may have predicted that would happen.

Molecules or atoms of solid metals are strongly attracted to one another. Even when heated, they jiggle back and forth through very tiny distances. As a result, they expand or contract very little when heated or cooled.

The table shows how much a 10-meter length of different solids expands

Solid	Amount a 10-m length expands when heated through 100°C
aluminum	2.3 cm
brass	1.8 cm
copper	1.7 cm
glass	1.7 cm
Pyrex glass	0.3 cm
gold	1.4 cm
iron	1.1 cm
platinum	0.9 cm
quartz	0.04 cm
silver	1.9 cm
steel	1.2 cm
zinc	2.5 cm

# of a Solid: An Explanation

when the temperature rises 100° Celsius (180° Fahrenheit). If engineers did not leave space between rails, the rails would buckle in hot weather.

Expansion of 10 meters of solid when heated

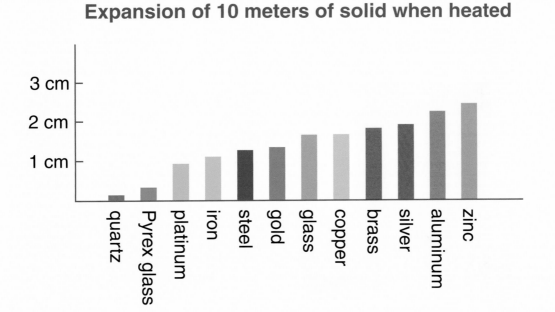

Ideas for Your Science Fair

* Build a model of a thermostat and explain how it works.
* Design another way to measure the expansion or contraction of a solid.

9. Layers of Liquids

Things you will need:
- ✓ short, wide jar
- ✓ rubbing alcohol
- ✓ red and blue food coloring
- ✓ coffee stirrer
- ✓ funnel
- ✓ cooking oil
- ✓ cold water
- ✓ liquid measuring cup

Some kinds of matter are more compact (denser) than others. Suppose you have two identical shoe boxes. You fill one with sand and the other with cotton balls. Even though the boxes are the same size, the box with sand weighs more. Sand is denser than cotton.

For the same amount of space, compact (dense) things weigh more than less compact ones. Compact materials, such as metals, sink in water. Less compact things, such as wood, float in water. Do different liquids have different densities?

Let's Find Out!

1 Pour rubbing alcohol into a short, wide jar until the jar is about one-quarter full. Add several drops of red food coloring. Stir with a coffee stirrer.

2 Place the end of a funnel on the bottom of the jar.

Slowly pour cooking oil into the funnel until the jar is about half full. Which liquid is on top?

③ In a liquid measuring cup, color some water with blue food coloring.

④ Again, put the end of the funnel on the bottom of the jar. Slowly pour the blue water into the funnel. Stop when the jar is three-quarters full.

⑤ From what you can see, which liquid is the most compact (dense)? Which liquid is least dense?

blue water

Layers of Liquids:

The three liquids formed three separate layers. Water was on the bottom and alcohol was on top. Cooking oil was between them. Suppose you have water, alcohol, and cooking oil. You weigh 100 mL (3½ oz) of each liquid. You would find that water weighs the most and alcohol weighs the least. Because water is more compact (denser) than cooking oil, it

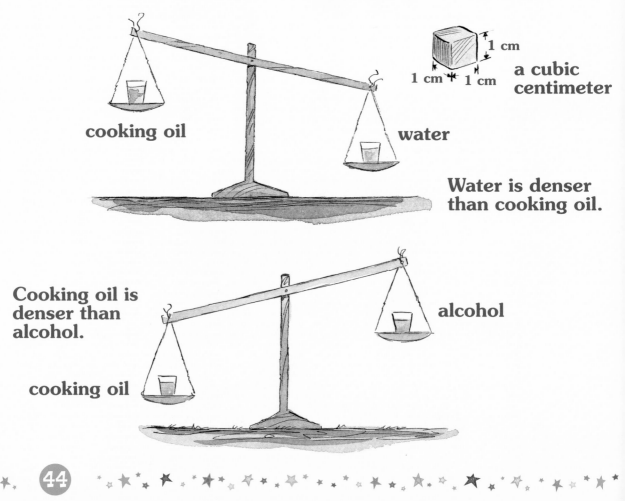

1 cm

1 cm   1 cm

a cubic centimeter

cooking oil

water

Water is denser than cooking oil.

Cooking oil is denser than alcohol.

alcohol

cooking oil

An Explanation

sinks in the oil. Alcohol is less compact (less dense) than cooking oil, so it floats on the oil.

The table shows substances with different densities.

The weight of 100 cubic centimeters of some common substances (g = grams).					
alcohol	79 g	aluminum	270 g	ice	91 g
gasoline	69 g	brass	850 g	glass	240–280 g
olive oil	92 g	copper	890 g	quartz	265 g
water	100 g	gold	1,930 g	oak wood	60–90 g
sea water	103 g	platinum	2,150 g	balsa wood	11–14 g

Ideas for Your Science Fair

★ Make multiple colored layers using salt solutions with different amounts of salt. Also use alcohol, cooking oil, water, milk, and other liquids.

★ Weigh equal volumes, say 100 mL, of water, cooking oil, and alcohol. Density is weight divided by volume. Calculate the density of each liquid.

★ Measure the density of some common solids.

Words to Know

carbon dioxide—A gas, denser than air, that does not burn. It can be used to put out fires.

cubic centimeter—A space that is one centimeter long, one centimeter wide, and one centimeter high.

density—The weight of a certain volume of a substance, such as the number of grams in one cubic centimeter.

evaporation—The change of a liquid to a gas.

gas—One of the three states of matter. It has no definite shape. It fills whatever container it is in.

heat—A form of energy that always flows from objects with a higher temperature to those with a lower temperature.

liquid—One of the three states of matter. It has a definite volume but takes the shape of the container it is in.

matter—Anything on earth that has weight and takes up space.

molecule—The smallest particle of a compound or element that can exist.

solid—One of the three states of matter. It has a definite size and shape. It cannot be compressed.

solution—A mixture of a solute and solvent that is the same throughout.

temperature—A measure of the "hotness" of something (the average speed of its molecules).

volume—The three-dimensional measurement of the space taken up by something.

Further Reading

Books

Ballard, Carol. *Solids, Liquids, and Gases: From Ice Cubes to Bubbles*. Chicago: Heinemann Library, 2004.

Bochinski, Julianne Blair. *The Complete Workbook for Science Fair Projects*. New York: John Wiley and Sons, 2004.

Dispezio, Michael A. *Super Sensational Science Fair Projects*. New York: Sterling Publishing, 2002.

Oxlade, Chris. *States of Matter*. Chicago: Heinemann Library, 2002.

Internet Addresses

Andrew Rader Studios. *Chem4kids.com*. "States of Matter." <http://www.chem4kids.com/files/matter_states.html>

MathMol. *What Is Matter?* © 1996. <http://www.nyu.edu/pages/mathmol/textbook/whatismatter.html>

Materials Research Society. *Strange Matter*. "Fun Stuff!" n.d. <http://www.strangematterexhibit.com/jump.html>

Index